Original title:
Inside the Walls of Love

Copyright © 2025 Creative Arts Management OÜ
All rights reserved.

Author: Simon Fairchild
ISBN HARDBACK: 978-1-80587-075-3
ISBN PAPERBACK: 978-1-80587-545-1

The Language of Touch

A wink that says, 'I'm hungry,'
A nudge that means 'Let's play.'
Tickles traded like secrets,
In this game, we've lost our way.

Hand in hand, we trip and tumble,
Your laugh like a cheerful bell.
Words are clumsy like our dance,
Touch, our language, speaks quite well.

A Chamber of Memories

In the drawer, socks lie mismatched,
Like my brain post-cuddle time.
Each laugh we stored, a sweet ticket,
To this rollercoaster rhyme.

Photographs in silly poses,
His hair a bird's nest, oh so grand.
Every frame, a blast of laughter,
Captured times, not quite as planned.

Quiet Confessions

Whispers draped like cozy blankets,
Guilty chuckles in the night.
Our secrets spill like soda pop,
Bubbles burst in pure delight.

Tick-tock goes the clock, we giggle,
Lights out, it's our little club.
Confessions shared with pizza slices,
In this hideaway, we rub-a-dub.

The Light in Your Eyes

Your gaze is like a disco ball,
Reflecting joy in every glance.
With mischief dancing in your pupils,
You make my heart do the cha-cha-chance.

Every cringe and every wink,
Turns the world to pure delight.
I stumble like a dorky kid,
But in your eyes, I take flight.

Whispers in the Heart's Sanctuary

In the corner, a sock did hide,
Its mate searched high, it searched wide.
Whispering secrets of laundry doom,
In the dryer, they share a room.

A pillow fight turns into a dance,
With feathery laughter, we take a chance.
Hearts collide, then burst into glee,
As we trip over slippers, one, two, three.

Echoes Beneath the Starlit Ceiling

Under twinkling lights, we make our bet,
To stay awake, not to forget.
But one wink leads to sleepy yawns,
While dreaming of breakfast with goofy fawns.

We craft silly stories, with laughter we weave,
Of dragons who cook and pirates naive.
With echoes of joy bouncing off the walls,
We plot escapades till the night softly calls.

Bound by the Threads of Affection

A quirky quilt stitched with care,
Holds stories of chaos and laughter rare.
Fabrications of moments snug and bright,
Each patch a memory, a giggle at night.

Knitting up trouble, we craft with flair,
With tangled yarn, we form a pair.
Bound tight in warmth, we share a wink,
With each silly stitch, we laugh and think.

The Secret Garden of Embrace

In our garden of giggles, the flowers bloom,
Each petal a pun, dispelling all gloom.
Bumblebees buzzing with jokes in flight,
We chase them around, what a comical sight!

A patch of daisies, a playful tease,
We pluck a few, make wishes with ease.
Petals fall softly, like laughter shared,
In this wild garden, love's giggle's declared.

Gentle Pulses of Belonging

In a cozy nook where laughs collide,
I trip on your shoelace, and you just glide.
Our giggles echo, bouncing off the floor,
Who knew a simple mishap could mean more?

With popcorn fights and pillow beams,
You steal my snacks while I plot your schemes.
The cat joins in, a furball of glee,
In this chaotic dance, just you and me.

Your socks on the sofa, my coffee cup flip,
Love's a circus, on this wild trip.
We toast to the moments that make us grin,
Like the time I thought you were a twin!

And here we are, full of quirky flair,
With you, every day feels light as air.
In our little world, silliness thrives,
Together we laugh, together we dive.

Roots of Affection

In the garden of quirky, where we both grow,
You water the plants while I steal the show.
With a spade in my hand, I dig up the past,
Finding treasures and laughs that just can't last.

The sun kisses petals, your sneakers in mud,
I slip on the rake, landing right with a thud.
You chuckle and ask, 'Did you dance with a root?'
I nod, wear my pride like a floppy-brimmed boot.

We plant seeds of humor, and laughter takes flight,
Watering dreams in the warm morning light.
Your puns are the fertilizer—oh so divine,
With you by my side, this garden will shine.

So let's grow our love, with the silliest flair,
Tending our patch with the utmost care.
In each quirk and giggle, our roots intertwine,
Forever entwined, oh how sweetly we pine.

The Fragrance of Forever

Socks on the floor, a trail I weave,
A scent of romance, who would believe?
Cooking together, a disaster in sight,
Gourmet or chaos? Both feel just right.

Bickering over, whose turn was it last?
The microwave beeping, a love song, so fast.
Pizza in hand, our laughter does spill,
In the kitchen of chaos, time stands still.

Tapestry of Souls Intertwined

Twisted like pretzels, our hearts do align,
Woven in mishaps that always define.
If you trip on my toes, it's a dance of delight,
Two left feet, but we're flying tonight.

Sharing the bed, with blankets galore,
Rolling like burritos, yet wanting more.
Sleepy-eyed giggles at the break of dawn,
In this wild tapestry, we're never withdrawn.

Glimmers of Joy in a Shared Horizon

Sunshine and giggles, a morning so bright,
Coffee-stained smiles as we share our plight.
In the car, you sing off-key with pride,
A duet of laughter, our joy will not hide.

Paint splattered walls, a canvas gone wild,
"Abstract" by choice, we're each other's child.
Each brushstroke a memory, in colors so bold,
In this shared horizon, our hearts never cold.

Breaths of Serenity in a Loving Nest

Gentle snoring, a symphony sweet,
Pillow fights flee as we flop to our feet.
Whiskers and fur, a cat on the prowl,
Together we laugh, as life makes us howl.

Chasing each other 'round corners anew,
Life in the chaos feels oh-so-true.
In the softest of moments, we bubble and burst,
In our cozy retreat, love's always immersed.

Veils of Trust in Hidden Rooms

In secret nooks where laughter lies,
We tell our jokes, and hope they rise.
With whispered truths by candle's glow,
Our hearts like rubber bands will grow.

Behind closed doors, the dance begins,
We twirl on floors made out of sins.
A comedy of errors plays,
As love becomes our silly craze.

Notes from the Chamber of Caresses

In softest corners, giggles cling,
We scribble notes on bathroom springs.
Each little poke, a playful tease,
In chambers where we feel at ease.

With sticky hands, we grab the snack,
We giggle as we share the pack.
Each crumb a secret, sweet delight,
We laugh together deep into the night.

Lanterns of Hope in the Night

We light our lamps with silly dreams,
And chase the dark with childish schemes.
Each flicker twirls, a dance of hope,
We tie balloons to love's bright rope.

Through shadowed paths, we skip and play,
Our lanterns guide us on our way.
With every wink and playful shout,
The warmth of love won't let us doubt.

The Language of Quiet Comfort

In whispers soft, our secrets flow,
Like breezy winds that gently blow.
We make each other blush and grin,
In quiet moments where we win.

Coffee cups and warm embraces,
The funny look on all our faces.
In silence, jokes are often shared,
A language fine, a love declared.

Hidden Corners of Desire

In the cupboard, snacks piled high,
We giggle as we reach for pie.
Your secret stash behind the door,
A playful hunt, forever more.

Silly whispers in the night,
We laugh until we see the light.
Under blankets, silly dreams,
Our hearts burst forth in joyous themes.

The quirky socks we wear askew,
A fashion choice, just me and you.
With each jest, our laughter blooms,
In corners tight, where love resumes.

Together through this maze we roam,
In every nook, we find our home.
Chasing shadows, side by side,
In love's embrace, we take the ride.

Reflections of Us

In the mirror, funny faces we make,
With each grin, more laughter we stake.
Your messy hair and my wild grin,
In these reflections, we always win.

We steal the covers, what a sight,
Fighting for warmth, our quirky fight.
With each shove and playful tease,
We find the comfort that never flees.

Dance parties in our socks, oh dear,
Twisting, turning, with joyous cheer.
In these moments, we truly shine,
With every step, our hearts entwine.

Each glance a spark, each laugh a song,
In this duet, where we belong.
With silly jokes and playful thrust,
Together, darling, it's a must.

Echoing Hearts

Your snoring echoes like a drum,
Yet in the night, I still feel fun.
A symphony of sleepy sighs,
In the quiet, laughter lies.

We share our dreams, both strange and bright,
With dinosaurs that take to flight.
A world created, just us two,
In echoes of love, there's always room.

Through whispered secrets, we conspire,
To build a castle, set afire.
In each heartbeat, a joyful dance,
With every glance, a loving chance.

Tumbling hearts in a playful race,
Chasing each other, we find our place.
In fleeting moments, we share our spark,
Together always, lighting the dark.

Tapestry of Shared Moments

A patchwork quilt of laugh and fun,
Each silly stitch, a tale begun.
From spilled coffee to late-night snacks,
We weave our stories, no lacks.

Your dance moves make the cat retreat,
But still, you rise, tapping your feet.
With every flail, my heart's in stitches,
In these fibers, love enriches.

Cooking chaos with burnt delight,
Your culinary skills take flight.
Yet in the kitchen, joy we find,
With every mishap, our hearts unwind.

In memories, we thread the past,
A tapestry we'll always cast.
With jokes and warmth, we stake our claim,
In shared moments, we play the game.

Cradled Dreams

In the land of mismatched socks,
We dance to the beat of funny clocks.
Coffee spills like love's sweet tease,
Laughter bubbles, puts hearts at ease.

Pillow fights, our nightly war,
Chasing dreams from corner to door.
Your snoring sounds like a cat in pain,
Yet somehow, I can't refrain from the gain.

In kitchen chaos, we try to bake,
Flour flying with every mistake.
You find my mixing skill quite a joke,
Yet together, we make the best broth to soak.

From silly selfies to goofy plays,
Each moment counts in our own way.
With a wink and a laugh, life's a scream,
In this home of ours, we truly dream.

A Haven of Hearts

We built a nest of mismatched chairs,
Frogs in tuxedos dance in pairs.
Bubble gum stuck to the floor,
Your giggles spill out; I demand more.

The cat thinks he's the lord of the house,
While you twirl around like a playful spouse.
Chasing shadows, we trip and fall,
Your laughter rings out, the best of all.

Our movies are a mix of old and new,
What's black and white? Just ask the zoo!
Popcorn fights and candy spills,
Sweet mischief thrives on our playful thrills.

As sunsets paint the room in gold,
We share secrets that can't be told.
With every glance, our world spins round,
In this haven, love's humor abounds.

Interwoven Destinies

You stole my fries without a care,
A bid for love, or just a dare?
With every glance, my laughter soars,
As you wiggle through life's open doors.

Matching socks? Now that's a myth,
Yet you wear mine while I laugh and quip.
Our stories twist in hilarious knots,
You're my partner in all the silly spots.

The world's a stage, our circus grand,
A tightrope of giggles, hand in hand.
With bloopers and burps, we play our parts,
Entangled fates, and interwoven hearts.

In this whirlwind, life feels just right,
Every blunder turns into a delight.
With your silly grin, I feel so free,
In this chaos, it's you and me.

The Canvas of Our Souls

With paint on fingers, we make our mark,
A masterpiece born from a giggling spark.
Doodles of dreams spread across the floor,
Each stroke a laugh, who could ask for more?

Foreseeing splatters, you sweep my feet,
In this gallery, we both compete.
Every canvas tells a funny tale,
Of pizza nights, and silly fails.

The fridge displays our best works of art,
Each failed recipe, a flavor chart.
With laughter echoing through our days,
Life's colors merge in delightful ways.

So let's paint this world with hues so bright,
Together we'll chase every splendid light.
With laughter as our brush, let's spin and sway,
Creating a love that forever will play.

Timeless Caresses

In the kitchen, your dance floor,
With pots and pans, we both galore.
You laugh, I trip, a slippery scene,
Love's choreography, quite the routine.

Mismatched socks, what a sight,
You're a rainbow, I'm a blight.
Yet we twirl, in colors wide,
A joyful mess, with hearts as guide.

Your snore is music, a symphony frail,
Each note a laugh, like love's own trail.
I pandaschlep as you mouse in dreams,
Tickling your feet, oh what a scheme.

Through silly fights, we make amends,
As fortunate as those with goldfish friends.
Together we grin, through thick and thin,
You spill the beans, and I just grin.

Echoes of Our Laughter

In the hall, your giggles ring,
Like a chorus, through everything.
With playful jests, we tease and jest,
A chuckle fest, our hearts are blessed.

You tripped on air, what a sight!
Both of us laughing, pure delight.
A place where we misplace our woes,
Like lost socks in a laundry prose.

The coffee spills, oh what a mess,
We paint the walls with our happiness.
Joyfully we dance, while chaos reigns,
With mismatched steps, in love's domains.

Each mishap a gem, a tapestry spun,
In our crazy world, we've already won.
Hand in hand, our laughter flows,
In the echoes, our affection grows.

Heartbeats in the Silence

In the quiet, you munch away,
Chips crunch loudly, that's your play.
I watch your smile, a silly grin,
A banquet for two, love's secret win.

Silent moments, they tickle my muse,
Your every sigh a playful ruse.
With our heartbeats set to a soft tune,
We share laughter beneath the moon.

Your secret snack stash, I must confess,
Each hidden treat causes such a mess.
Yet here, in silence, we bubble and brew,
Beneath layers of jest, my heart beats for you.

With soft glances, like quicksilver streams,
In unspoken words, we build our dreams.
In this hush, our love's a play,
A joyful jest, in our silly way.

The Refuge of Your Smile

The clouds may darken, rains may pour,
Yet your grin, I can't ignore.
You're my refuge, my sunbeam bright,
Sorting through storms, with pure delight.

Even when the world's a mess,
Your laugh rescues my distress.
With silly faces and monkey charms,
You wrap me safe in warmth and arms.

You spill my drink, and I just sigh,
But then you wink, oh my, oh my!
In playful chaos, we stand quite tall,
My heart's safe haven, in love's own hall.

With a tilt of your head and a pouting face,
You turn every mistake into a fun embrace.
Laughter shared, our hearts entwine,
A joyful refuge, together divine.

A Symphony of Untold Intimacies

In a room filled with socks and old shoes,
We dance like fools, ignoring the clues.
Mismatched rhythms in a playful affair,
Twisting and turning, without a care.

The cat looks on, judging our sway,
As we giggle and trip, making our way.
Laughter echoes, a sweet serenade,
In the symphony of mess we've made.

Whispers turn into silly old pranks,
As we count the moments, and give our thanks.
The pizza rolls burn, but we don't mind,
In this jumbled love, joy is well-defined.

Amidst the chaos, love's song is clear,
With every misstep, we pull each other near.
In the notes of our heart, we find the beat,
A funny dance that can't be beat.

The Calm Following Tender Storms

After thundercracks of misunderstood words,
We wear silly hats as peace is stirred.
Rainbows peek out from the clouds we drew,
As laughter emerges with every view.

Holding hands through the gales we made,
With funny faces that never quite fade.
We dance on puddles, splashing our woes,
In the aftermath, love only grows.

A playful truce in the kitchen's embrace,
We cook up chaos at our own pace.
The blender yells, our apron doth fly,
In this gentle chaos, we reach for the sky.

Tender storms pass, yet leave us giddy,
In this calm that follows, we're quite the witty.
Love's a laugh, a game for two,
In every moment, I'm glad I'm with you.

Paths of Sacrifice in the Garden of Us

We planted dreams in a garden so wild,
With love as our soil, and laughter as mild.
We traded shovels for some ice cream bars,
And watered our hopes under candy-filled stars.

Weeding out worries with giggles and charm,
In the chaos of flowers, we find our calm.
Sacrifices made with snacks on the side,
In our whimsical garden, love is our guide.

As flowers bloom, so do our quirks,
In the pathways of joy, our laughter lurks.
We chase down squirrels for stealing our fruit,
Wearing silly hats like a couple of brutes.

We stroll through rows of mismatched delights,
In our patch of affection, everything excites.
The garden is wild, but our hearts stay true,
In the paths we've paved, it's just me and you.

The Hidden Alcove of Acceptance

In the corners of life, where oddities lie,
We find our groove as the days slip by.
With mismatched socks and a shared ice cream,
We celebrate quirks, oh, how we beam!

Your silly jokes, they lift me up high,
While we nap on a couch with a cat — oh my!
In the alcove of love, we make our pact,
Every flaw embraced, nothing we lack.

The world spins fast while we paint our dreams,
In the sticky moments, nothing's as it seems.
We dance with laughter through thick and thin,
In acceptance, my dear, it's a total win.

So let's build our fort with pillows and glee,
Creating a space where we can just be.
In this hidden alcove, we thrive like a tree,
In the comedy of love, just you and me.

Secrets Beneath the Surface

Whispers dance where hearts reside,
Hidden giggles, a secret tide.
Behind each smile, a playful tease,
Laughter floats upon the breeze.

Socks mismatched, yet hearts aligned,
Jokes exchanged, our love defined.
Between the walls, we laugh and play,
In our own quirky ballet.

Chasing dreams on a lopsided track,
Who knew romance could be so wack?
With every laugh, the world's a show,
Two jesters dance, stealing the glow.

In our fort, beneath a blanket sky,
We craft our tales, oh me, oh my!
Secrets buried, no need to hide,
In these hearts, our joys collide.

The Sanctuary of Affection

Cuddles cozy in a pillow fight,
Tickles shared until daylight.
Pasta flung with a twist of fate,
Our messy love, it's never late.

Dancing socks across the floor,
Every step opens a door.
Chasing silence with laughter's call,
Our sanctuary, a quirky hall.

Cupcake icing on the nose,
A pastry war? Who really knows!
Sticky fingers, sweet delight,
This rhythm feels so right.

Shall we build a fort today?
Where cheesy jokes come out to play?
A castle made of love and cream,
Here, we fulfill our wildest dream.

Shadows of Longing

Behind the curtain, a whisper breathes,
The chuckle soft, as laughter weaves.
With every glance, a playful spark,
Shadows teasing in the dark.

Tangled sheets and stolen glances,
In this dance, our heart advances.
A wink, a nod, a silly face,
In this game, we've found our place.

Wishing well but laughing too,
Who knew longing could feel so blue?
Yet in the night, our giggles sway,
A harmony that leads the way.

Footsteps echo, secrets hold,
Stories shared, both young and old.
In shadows cast, love finds a way,
Tickling hearts, come what may.

A Garden of Sighs

In a garden where flowers bloom,
Laughter echoes, dispelling gloom.
With every sigh, a petal falls,
Our hearts giggle within these walls.

Honeyed words like bees at play,
Buzzing dreams and puns display.
Strolling paths of daffodil light,
Each turn, another funny sight.

Giggles sprout from roots of cheer,
In this haven, love is clear.
Chasing rabbits, dreams take flight,
In our garden, the world feels right.

Underneath the lemon tree,
Silly tales just you and me.
With every chuckle, hearts entwine,
In this space, our smiles shine.

In the Company of Dreams

In dreams we dance on jellybeans,
With twinkling stars and silly scenes.
We ride on clouds, so fluffy and bright,
Chasing the moon till the morning light.

A penguin waltzes, a cat plays drums,
We're making laughs, forgetting thumbs.
Unicorns sipping cocoa with glee,
In this dreamland, we're all so free.

The Sanctuary of Us

In our castle made of marshmallow fluff,
We wear crowns of chocolate—tasty, but tough.
Our laughter echoes like a bouncing ball,
As we snack on cupcakes, we're giants tall.

The cat's our knight, with a feathery plume,
While the dog guards treasures in our sweet room.
We build paper forts, defend from the rain,
In this silly realm, there's never a bane.

A Diary of Heartstrings

Once I wrote a love letter to cheese,
It laughed at my rhymes, just aiming to tease.
With every cheesy line, my heart would flutter,
But then I dropped it in peanut butter.

I scribbled more tales of donuts and pies,
Spelling with sprinkles—an artist's surprise.
Each page a giggle, each word a delight,
My diary's full of sweet, silly sights.

The Tidal Flow of Feelings

Feelings splash like waves on the shore,
A fish in a tuxedo? What's more to explore!
We ride on currents, on lollipops made,
The ocean's our playground, in sunshine we wade.

Tickles from dolphins, they dance with grace,
Waves crashing softly, like a pillowcase.
With laughter constellations all over the sea,
In this watery world, we're as happy as can be.

Embers of Devotion

In the kitchen, pots do clang,
Spaghetti flying, oh what a bang!
You said, "I cook with flair and style,"
But burnt toast makes me run a mile.

Your socks are missing, lost in the fold,
Under the couch or so I'm told.
You laugh and say it's a treasure hunt,
Next time I'll label, but that's my front!

Dog steals my sandwich, won't let it go,
You giggle, saying, "That's love, you know!"
We'll chase him with glee, a silly race,
Then sit on the floor, no time to waste.

Each day is chaos, a comical scene,
With you, dear heart, life's a routine.
Through laughter, we find our joyful tune,
A dance in the kitchen, under the moon.

The Celestial Embrace

Starry nights with you by my side,
In your gaze, I want to hide.
You point at constellations above,
But I can't find my one true love.

Your snoring sounds like a space rocket,
I swear I'm rooming with a socket.
You dream of planets, I dream of sleep,
Counting sheep while you softly beep.

The coffee spills, a cosmic mess,
You grin and say, "It's part of the test!"
I laugh, your playful, sleepy grin,
In our universe, there's no loss or win.

With every blunder, we make it right,
Orbiting each other, day and night.
In this galaxy, we're quite the pair,
A love comically beyond compare.

Melodies of Intimacy

You hit the notes, but hit the wrong key,
Playing the tune of love's melody.
I dance like a fool, but you don't mind,
Two awkward souls, hilariously aligned.

Your shower singing, so offbeat and bold,
Turns the mundane into stories retold.
I join in the chorus, voices a clash,
Creating moments where giggles flash.

Our playlists mix, your pop with my rock,
A symphony made of jumbled talk.
In every beat, our hearts collide,
A comedy show we can't seem to hide.

Through laughter and music, we find the way,
In rhythm and rhyme, come what may.
Our love is a song, a light-hearted tune,
Dancing through life, morning to noon.

Canvas of Our Dreams

With brushes in hand, we paint our days,
You splash the colors in wild arrays.
I step in the puddle, oh what a sight,
We giggle and laugh, what a delight!

Your portraits of me look quite absurd,
A nose that's too big and hair like a bird.
But every stroke tells a tale so true,
In our funny world, nothing's askew.

Masterpieces made from spilled red wine,
An abstract art that's truly divine.
Each canvas a glimpse of life's sweet jest,
In this gallery of love, we are blessed.

The frames may falter, the colors may run,
But in this chaos, we've truly won.
With you, dear artist, life's all aglow,
In the art of our love, the joy does flow.

A Haven Built on Gentle Promises

In a house of socks and mismatched pairs,
We dance around the daily flares.
Spilled coffee on my favorite chair,
You laugh it off without a care.

With post-it notes on every wall,
You scribble love, I drool and sprawl.
Our cat's the judge of it all,
Giving a nod when we start to fall.

The fridge is stocked with odd delights,
Leftover pizza from late-night bites.
Your cooking, like my dance, ignites,
An adventure every weekend night.

In this kingdom of our kooky whims,
We've mastered juggling, despite the grim.
Each moment's sweet, a playful hymn,
Together we shine, our light won't dim.

The Rhythm of Echoed Heartbeats

Your heart beats like a monkey's call,
In sync with mine, a wild brawl.
We trip on dreams, we make 'em fall,
Laughing loudly through it all.

In the kitchen, our dance floor's tight,
Every trip's a chance for flight.
Spinning pasta, oh what a sight,
We laugh at dinners gone awry tonight.

Bedtime stories become our jest,
In haunted tales, we find the best.
Monsters knock but we won't rest,
Pillow fights ensure we're blessed.

With echoes of our silly tales,
Life is bright; it never fails.
We've built a ship that always sails,
Through goofy dreams, we write our gales.

Secrets Carved into the Surface of Us

In the bark of trees, we carved our names,
Amidst the laughter and silly games.
Whispers traded, no one claims,
Our secrets hide in wild flames.

Your quirks are gems, a treasure chest,
Hiccups come, we laugh the best.
Every wrong turn is a jest,
Together we thrive, we've been so blessed.

Underneath the stars, pillow dreams,
We count the jokes, or so it seems.
With comet tails and crazy beams,
Laughter echoes, or so it gleams.

In every crack, a story's spun,
Two clowns at heart, we've just begun.
Chasing rainbows, just for fun,
In every pulse, our hearts are one.

Nests of Kindness by the Hearth

By the fire, we toss our fears,
Roasting marshmallows, sipping beers.
Your silly stories bring me cheers,
In this nest, it's love that steers.

With cozy blankets wrapped around,
Crazy cat jumps, it's jumping ground.
You sing off-key, but love's the sound,
In this haven, joy is found.

Chasing shadows as daylight wanes,
We twirl in socks, we make the gains.
Life's a play, we've got no chains,
In laughter's echo, our love reigns.

The windows rattle, but so do we,
In a wacky waltz, our jubilee.
Nestled tight, just you and me,
By the hearth, we're always free.

Illuminated Hearts

When you steal the fries from my plate,
I laugh and say it's fate!
Our love's a game, a playful jest,
You know I think you're the best.

In the kitchen, we dance around,
Burnt toast and laughter abound.
Your cooking, a chaotic spree,
But there's nowhere I'd rather be.

With socks that clash and mismatched shoes,
We argue over silly views.
Yet through each quirk, each little fight,
Your smile makes everything right.

We share a world of silly cheers,
Where laughter rolls like happy tears.
In this playful mess, we thrive,
With love that makes our hearts come alive.

A Paradise of Emotions

Your snoring like a freight train's sound,
But in this chaos, joy is found.
We fight for blankets, steal the heat,
My heart warms every time we meet.

Like dancing ducks upon the lawn,
Our silly days, they just go on.
We wear our quirks like badges bright,
Making every moment light.

You hide my keys, I lose my shoe,
Each lost item brings laughter anew.
In this circus, you're the best act,
Your charm is such a perfect fact.

With ticklish fights and giggles loud,
In our little world, I'm so proud.
This paradise is laughter's tune,
Together, we'll dance under the moon.

Gardens of Affectionate Shadows

In the garden, we plant our dreams,
Where sunlight dances, and laughter beams.
Your jokes can grow the tallest trees,
With blossoms swaying in the breeze.

You trip on petals, fall with grace,
Your goofy charm lights up the place.
We chase butterflies and might just find,
A secret world where hearts unwind.

We hide in bushes, play peek-a-boo,
Every giggle draws me closer to you.
Whimsical thoughts tumble and roll,
In the garden, you capture my soul.

With frolicking sun, till twilight calls,
Our love unfolds within these walls.
With every laugh and gentle tease,
We blossom together, hearts at ease.

The Magic of Together

With socks on backwards, you begin the show,
A dance that causes hearts to glow.
You trip and giggle, eyes so bright,
In this chaos, oh what a sight!

Magic brews in spilled popcorn,
On movie nights, we laugh 'til dawn.
Your jokes are like a comet's flight,
Soaring high, with pure delight.

Every mishap turns into a tale,
As we ride on friendship's sail.
In this playful swirl of mirth,
We find our magic, our true worth.

With starlit skies and whispers soft,
In every moment, our spirits loft.
Together we create our song,
In the laughter where we belong.

Shades of Connection in Quiet Moments

In the quiet, we often grin,
Your snort is like a trumpet's din.
We sip our tea and spill the beans,
While plotting pranks behind the screens.

With each wink, a new idea flares,
Our laughter bouncing off the chairs.
You say I dance like I'm a duck,
But I'll outsmart you — guess my luck!

We mug for selfies, faces wide,
A joyride on life's silly ride.
In every glance, a bond so sweet,
We trade our secrets, laughter's treat.

Underneath that quiet shade,
We craft our world, a grand charade.
With smirks and puns, we build our home,
A place where joy is free to roam.

The Bridge of Every Shared Sunrise

Each morning brings a brand new game,
Your bedhead's wild — oh, what a claim!
Together we fight for coffee's touch,
Like warrior pros — we need it much.

You trip on socks, I stumble too,
A wobbly dance in morning dew.
We make a pact, today we win,
Then spill our drinks — let chaos begin!

The sun peeks in with a playful wink,
We plot our day while on the brink.
You call me silly, I throw a pie,
Who knew that food can really fly?

As we bridge our laughter and our quirks,
The world beyond just calmly lurks.
Together, dear, we'll chase the run,
On sunlit paths, we laugh and run.

Whispers in the Heart

With every whisper, jokes unfold,
Your giggles warm me more than gold.
In candlelight, we share our dreams,
While plotting silly, wild schemes.

You whisper softly, "Was that a joke?"
I nod and grin — how we evoke!
Between the laughs and playful jive,
Together, dear, we feel alive.

In cozy chats and secret glances,
We pull each other into dances.
Like shadows creeping, dreams we dare,
In these whispers, we bloom a pair.

With every giggle, my heart does cheer,
In your laughter, I find my sphere.
Through every joke, a love that starts,
Whispers echo deep in hearts.

Echoes of Tenderness

With echoes soft, your voice does charm,
You tease my socks, but mean no harm.
In goofy breaths, we share our glee,
A space where silly runs so free.

Each nudge's a spark, igniting fun,
Two hearts in sync — we're quite a pun!
You hide behind the fridge for kicks,
While I pretend to dodge your tricks.

In this dance of tender plays,
We love and laugh through all our days.
Your warmth a blanket, soft and wide,
Together here, our joys collide.

With echoes sweet, we fill our hall,
A symphony of love — our call.
From whispered jokes to gentle cheers,
In every laugh, we calm our fears.

The Rhythm of Togetherness

We two dance like penguins in the night,
Bumping into walls, oh what a sight!
With laughter echoing off the floor,
Two left feet? We'll just ask for more.

Baking cookies, flour everywhere,
Sugar on noses, a sweet love affair.
Burnt the toast, but who really cares?
We'll feast on laughter, served with some stares.

Tangoing through small kitchen spaces,
Dodging the dog and silly grimaces.
We giggle as we trip on a shoe,
In our own world, just us two.

Every battle fought with playful glee,
Competing for who can find the remote, you see.
With popcorn fights and movie debates,
Our silly rhythm never hesitates.

Cherished Whispers

In the quiet corners, we share our dreams,
Almonds in pillows, oh how it seems!
Your snoring, my tunes, quite the duet,
A melody mixed with a hint of regret.

Whispers of secrets, all cluttered and neat,
Your socks on the floor, oh, what a feat!
Mismatched pairs in a loving embrace,
Searching for warmth in this wacky space.

Grocery lists and half-eaten pies,
Outrageous plans and exaggerated lies.
Underneath starlight, we sketch our fate,
Finding laughter in the chaos we create.

In chaotic moments, you are my muse,
With you, my love, there's nothing to lose.
Together we'll make a raucous noise,
Our whispers crafted with silly poise.

The Infinite Embrace

Wrapped in your arms, a blanket of fun,
Like two silly kittens caught in the sun.
Your goofy grin ignites a spark,
Together we shine, even in the dark.

Tangled in sheets, a comedy show,
Playing charades with a puppy in tow.
Laughter erupts, it fills the air,
In our embrace, we've nary a care.

Your laugh is like music, a jolly good tune,
Floating on bubbles beneath a bright moon.
With tickles and jests, we sway with grace,
In this infinite hug, we've found our place.

The world may spin outside our door,
But here we are, forever wanting more.
With goofy antics and love's delight,
We juggle our joy through day and night.

Ephemeral Soirees

In tiny moments, we throw grand affairs,
With cereal dinners and mismatched chairs.
Sipping on soda from fancy old glass,
Waltzing through chaos, oh what a class!

Sticky hands from candy galore,
Dancing on counters, then down to the floor.
We feast on nostalgia, the night never ends,
A whimsical gathering of two best friends.

Our laughter's contagious, it spills through the air,
Conducting a symphony without a care.
With silly hats on and outrageous flair,
Every heartbeat is bliss, rich beyond compare.

These soirees are fleeting, like dreams in the night,
Yet in every chuckle, you feel the light.
So raise your glass high, let the good times unfurl,
In this dance of delight, you are my world.

The Bridge of Understandings

We danced on beams of awkward fate,
Where every stumble made us relate.
Your laugh would echo, a sweet delight,
As we navigated love's silly fight.

In shoes too big, we wobbled through,
With secret whispers and random to-do.
You said my jokes were top-tier absurd,
I laughed so hard, I lost my word.

Each word we shared, a puzzle piece,
With laughter the glue, we never cease.
We built our bridge with bits of cheer,
A wacky world, with you my dear.

So let's cross the gaps, hand in hand,
In this playful love, we boldly stand.
No serious ties, just a funny bind,
In the bridge of understanding we find.

Tides of Our Bond

Oh, love is like a wobbly boat,
Drifting through waves, we happily float.
You splash me with jokes; I throw a grin,
In each playful jab, we reel love in.

The tide may pull, but we just laugh,
In our sea of quirks, we craft our path.
Surfboards of hope, we ride the crest,
Amidst the froth, it's you I invest.

With every wave, new jokes arise,
As we chase sunsets and giggle surprise.
Your puns are like shells, washed on the shore,
Collecting smiles, I always want more.

In the currents, we sway and twirl,
You're the fishy queen of my goofy world.
In this sea of love, there's no need to grieve,
With our tidal bond, we've got tricks up our sleeve.

Beneath the Velvet Sky

Stargazing beneath a blanket of blue,
You said, "That star looks like my shoe!"
We laughed till our sides felt like they'd burst,
In this cosmic jest, our hearts rehearsed.

Moonlight tickled our silly dreams,
As shadows danced with mischievous beams.
You whispered tales of spacey delight,
While I pretended to reach for the night.

With every twinkle, a story spun,
In this velvet night, we both are one.
You're the comet that stole my heart,
In the galaxy of jokes, we'll never part.

So let's shoot for the stars, a playful chase,
In the laughter of cosmos, we find our place.
Underneath these skies with funny flair,
Our love's a journey; it's cosmic, I swear!

Enchanted by Your Presence

You walked in like a whirlwind of glee,
Casting spells with your humor spree.
Each grin you tossed, a charm so bright,
In your enchanting glow, everything's right.

With your mischievous wink, you pulled me near,
In this magic realm, there's nothing to fear.
Your puns are potions, bubbling with fun,
A cauldron of laughter, we've only begun.

In the forest of quirks, hand in hand,
Every leafy giggle, we understand.
We're wizards of joy in a straight jacket of time,
Mixing our quirks, creating our rhyme.

So let's dance in this clicking spell,
With every belly laugh, we cast it well.
Enchanted by you, this playful scheme,
Together we weave the tapestry of dream.

Shadows that Dance in Tender Spaces

In corners where giggles often bloom,
We share our secrets, not a hint of gloom.
With socks on our hands, we tap on the floor,
Twisting and turning, begging for more.

A misstep here leads to laughter's boost,
As we bump and tumble, becoming deduced.
Your face in the mirror, a wig on my head,
We laugh till we ache, the tears almost shed.

In the light of the fridge, we snack side by side,
You reach for the salsa; I try to hide.
With chips in our laps and crumbs on our nose,
In this silly dance, our love forever grows.

So here's to the moments we often misplay,
To the joys we've created, come what may.
For every mishap, it's laughter we release,
In our tiny universe, we find our peace.

A Mosaic of Hearts Unseen

We paint our life with colors so bright,
In mismatched socks, we cause quite a sight.
With pancake flops that land on the floor,
You laugh so hard, you snort—oh, what's in store!

Every giggle's a note in our carefree tune,
While we dance through the kitchen, beneath the bright moon.
Spilling coffee like artists on a spree,
Creating a canvas, just you and me.

A cat on the counter, a dog in your lap,
A family circus, no time for a nap.
You juggle the fruit; I catch a pineapple,
Laughter erupts, our bond undeniable.

In this wacky gallery, our hearts intertwine,
Through the silliest moments, our love's well-defined.
With every day's chaos, we find humor's grace,
In the grand masterpiece, we share this space.

Fragments of Us in Every Corner

In hallways adorned with memories rare,
We trip over shoes, but we just don't care.
Your goofy grin lights up the dark,
As we play hide and seek, pretending to spark.

Fridge magnets that tell our unspoken tales,
Of battles with veggies and curious snails.
Each snippet of laughter sewn into our quilt,
Is a patchwork of love, a fabric we built.

With mismatched puzzles and socks on the bed,
You tease me with stories, which we both have shed.
In every little fragment, giggles abide,
As we chase down the moments, our joy our guide.

In corners where whispers and smiles combine,
We find our own rhythm, simply divine.
With every odd moment, our hearts take flight,
Creating a world where everything's right.

The Portrait of Togetherness

In a cozy nook, where giggles collide,
We sketch our own story, with joy as our guide.
Your paintbrush twirls, adding humor and glee,
While I dabble in colors that mimic the sea.

Butterfly coffee spills turn into art,
With splatters and laughter joining each part.
Our canvas is rich, with brush strokes of fate,
In frames overflowing, we happily create.

From awkward high-fives to mischief's embrace,
We create our own portrait, a warm little place.
With crayons and markers, we color the wild,
Our masterpiece grows, unrefined and styled.

So here's to the strokes of pure whimsy and fun,
In this wacky world, there's room for everyone.
With love painted brightly across every edge,
We celebrate together, we're happy, we pledge.

The Igloo of Solace

In a cozy igloo, we share a laugh,
Ice cubes clink while we sip on a half.
Penguins push, snowflakes swirl,
Together we dance, in a snowy whirl.

Laughter echoes, it fills the space,
Chilling moments, yet warm embrace.
Hot cocoa spills as we try to glide,
Frosty adventures with you as my guide.

Mittens tangled, faces aglow,
Falling backward, we play in the snow.
Giggles escape, we throw snowballs,
Love's a snowstorm, it never stalls!

In our igloo, the outside world's grey,
Here's to moments, where silliness stays.
Together we waffle, let laughter enthrall,
In this frosty castle, we have it all.

The Essence of Together

In our mismatched socks, we start the day,
Coffee spills on the floor—what a cliché!
Smiles and giggles make the morning bright,
We dance 'round the kitchen, what a sight!

You burn the toast, I laugh with glee,
Coffee cup juggling? That's a new spree.
We tackle the chores, a domestic spree,
Turning mundane into comedy.

Laundry tossed like confetti, what a blast,
As we race to finish, it's a silly contest.
Your sock finds my shirt, oh what a match!
In this messy love, there's no need to patch.

Together we twirl in chaos and fun,
Every mishap becomes a pun.
In tiny moments, our joys grow vast,
In this essence of us, we'll forever last.

Forgotten Epistles of Love

Love letters tucked in a shoe box high,
Whispers of sweetness, oh me, oh my!
Scribbled on napkins, ideas quite grand,
I typed with my heart, not quite with my hand.

Tiny envelopes stuck in the drawer,
Ink smudged from a pen, oh what a chore!
Each note a treasure, a memory's bliss,
In smeared ink love, there's always a twist.

You read my ramblings, then laugh at the lines,
'You really thought I liked pickles on fries?'
With every quirk, our laughter does swell,
In forgotten epistles, there's magic to tell.

So here's to the notes that we might have missed,
Our love's a comic, a delightful twist.
In quirky love letters, we navigate time,
In laughter and joy, there's rhythm and rhyme.

Secrets in the Moonlight

Under the stars, we share silly tales,
How you lost your shirt, while chasing the snails.
Moonbeams giggle, they whisper and sway,
In nighttime's embrace, let's play and play.

We plot secret missions, with giggles and glee,
To sneak snacks after bed, oh, can that be?
With shadows as allies, we dance on the lawn,
In the madness of night, till the break of dawn.

Fireflies tease us, they twinkle and dart,
Guiding our laughter, igniting the heart.
In this magical moment, with secrets we share,
Life's a funny story—fun's in the air!

So let's hold hands, in laughter we'll bask,
In moonlit secrets, let's shed every mask.
Together we shine, like stars in the night,
In this quirky romance, everything feels right.

Living in the Echo

In a home of echoes, we laugh and we play,
My socks disappear, but I'm still here to stay.
You hide the remote, and steal all my fries,
Yet your silly antics are my favorite surprise.

We dance in the hallway, with cat paws in sight,
Twisting and twirling, it's quite a delight.
Your giggles are music, oh sweet serenade,
As I step on the cat, and our plans start to fade.

In the chaos of laughter, we muddle each day,
With love that's contagious, it brightens the way.
From socks in the dryer to pizza-stained walls,
This home of ours echoes through all of its halls.

So here's to the moments we cherish and crown,
When laughter's the treasure, the world upside down.
Through whispers and smirks, we find our true bliss,
In our quirky love story, how could we miss?

Symphony of Lovers

We waltz in the kitchen, a sauce-splattered scene,
Your spatula strikes as we're caught in between.
A duet of chaos, with flour in the air,
Our culinary dreams made a mess everywhere.

You sing off-key, like a cat in a shoe,
While I serenade with a spoon as my crew.
Our hearts beat in rhythm, though the oven's a mess,
In this tender duet, it's chaos, not stress.

With laughter as trumpets and giggles as drums,
We dance like the wild, with no fear of the crumbs.
Through burnt bits of toast and spilled sugar trails,
Our love is the symphony that never quite fails.

So here's to our concerts in mismatched attire,
Each note of your laughter lifts me ever higher.
In this grand orchestra, we play side by side,
With you as my conductor, what a joyous ride!

The Aroma of Shared Smiles

With coffee in hand, you steal all the cream,
Each sip brings a giggle, we laugh as we dream.
Your morning hairdo, a wild tangled sight,
But it adds to the charm, you're my morning delight.

In the kitchen, we bake, with flour in our hair,
A recipe's disaster, we hardly can share.
But the scent of those cookies twirls sweet through the air,

As we break them so fast, like we haven't a care.

Sniffing your laughter, it's my favorite scent,
A park full of daisies, each moment well spent.
With your jokes and your puns, we giggle and sigh,
In this aromatic bliss, time simply flies by.

So here's to our mornings, a delightful routine,
With smiles as our seasoning, life's ever so keen.
In this fragrant affair, we savor each day,
Together we munch, in our silly buffet!

Along the Path of Wishes

We stroll hand in hand, with wishes in tow,
As you whisper my secrets to the flowers that grow.
The frogs start to croak, perfectly out of tune,
While we giggle at turtles that dance to the moon.

With stars in our eyes, and dreams on the breeze,
We trip on the path, but we laugh with such ease.
Each stumble a story, a bump on the scene,
Our wishes are sprinkled like glittery sheen.

The trees sway above, giving blessing's embrace,
While squirrels plot heists in this magical space.
With each silly moment, our hearts start to glow,
As we chase shooting stars with a comical flow.

So here's to our journey, with wishes we share,
A trail lined with laughter, and joys in the air.
As we prance through the night, with dreams like a song,
In the merriment of wishes, we always belong.

Stories Woven in Silk and Time

In a quilt of laughter, we reside,
Every thread a tale that's bona fide.
A sock once lost, though really quite shy,
Found in the arms of a hungry pie.

Tickles and giggles beneath the sun,
A dance in the kitchen, oh what fun!
Spaghetti mishaps, sauce on the floor,
Life's silly moments we can't ignore.

Wrapped in stories, our hearts entwined,
With each little mishap, joy we find.
Pillow fights end with feigned defeat,
In this cozy chaos, we feel complete.

Time flies like toast, it's quick and toast-ally,
Yet every laugh echoes so heartily.
Silly antics frame our golden days,
As love weaves fun in whimsical ways.

Reflections on a Warm Altar

With quirky mugs of coffee near,
Every sip brings you closer, my dear.
The couch becomes our sacred ground,
Where silly secrets are fiercely found.

Whiskers of kittens and feet in the air,
A dance with a broom, oh what a flare!
Shoes left scattered like thoughts in our mind,
A treasure hunt's joy that feels so refined.

Beaming laughter before the soft glow,
In the corners where our memories flow.
A mess of cuddles and crumbs we share,
In this funny chapel, love is laid bare.

Under a blanket, we slip and we slide,
Every chuckle, the giggle rides.
Ripples of joy on this altar so warm,
In our sanctuary, we weather the storm.

The Embrace that Knows No End

In a hug that stretches wide and free,
We twirl like leaves from that old oak tree.
A dance with your elbow, a waltz with a knee,
Who knew affection could be so silly?

Cartwheeling thoughts as we roll on the floor,
Every tumble shows love has a score.
The bed a trampoline, laughter takes flight,
In this ridiculous realm, we delight.

With every tickle, love grows even grand,
A wrist in a cuddle, it's so well planned.
Spin in the kitchen, pots racing too,
In this wacky world, I'm stuck like glue.

Laughter's the language of our sweet escape,
Every moment spicy, a dazzling shape.
Embraces that stretch way beyond just two,
In this dance of joy, it's me and you.

Comforts in the Silences Between

In quiet moments, our hearts still snicker,
An inside joke, it couldn't be slicker.
A smirk on your face, cheeky and bright,
In silence, we find a delightful light.

Paths of our minds take us far away,
To a land of dreams where the sillies play.
Miming our thoughts like performers we are,
Cracks of laughter echo, a cosmic bazaar.

Whiskers make their way through the quiet space,
Chasing shadows, it's a goofy race.
Our hearts begin giggling when nothing is said,
In the silence, love grows, like socks on your bed.

As stars blink softly and the night drifts near,
The smiles we share bring nothing to fear.
In every pause, without a word spoken,
Are the threads of humor that gently unbroken.

The Nest of Us

In a cozy spot, we both reside,
With popcorn fights, and laughter wide.
You steal my fries, I take your book,
Yet with a grin, we share a look.

The cat's our boss, she runs the show,
While we're just puppets, don't you know?
We dance to tunes from offbeat charts,
Creating chaos, and goofy arts.

Your coffee's cold, my toast is burnt,
We laugh about it, undeterred, unturned.
In this nest, absurd and sweet,
Every quirk's a charming treat.

We build our dreams on shaky ground,
With funny moments all around.
In this little nook, we're never alone,
In our wild world, we've made a home.

Moonlit Reveries

Beneath the stars, we pluck the night,
With silly songs and pillow fights.
You claim the moon, I seize the stars,
In our cosmos without cars.

Wearing our helmets made of socks,
We travel roads that have no blocks.
A sandwich here, a giggle there,
Adventurous crumbs float in the air.

You trip on dreams, I leap on sighs,
With laughter echoing through the skies.
No maps needed for this ride,
Just you and me, our hearts as guides.

In moonlit laughter, we concoct schemes,
Mixing reality with our dreams.
In these moments, so blissfully absurd,
We find our magic, undeterred.

Beneath the Tender Sky

Under the sun, our shadows play,
As you steal my hat, then run away.
In this dance of fun, we spin around,
Where silly giggles are always found.

Chasing clouds and squirrels too,
Every day a surprise or two.
With messy hair and mismatched clothes,
Our happiness oddly grows.

We build a fort from colorful sheets,
With dragon snacks and funny feats.
In our kingdom where laughter reigns,
Chaos is bliss, my heart explodes.

The sun may set, but we don't mind,
For in our joy, the world's aligned.
In the tender sky, where we belong,
We dance our dance, we sing our song.

The Pulse of Our Journey

With every step, a silly dance,
You twirl around, I take a chance.
In this journey, wild and bright,
Our laughter echoes through the night.

With mismatched shoes and half-tied laces,
We wander through the craziest places.
When maps betray, we just improvise,
While chasing butterflies that never lie.

Your ridiculous tales, they charm my ears,
As we laugh away all our silly fears.
In this pulsing rhythm, we find our way,
Where every bump makes us laugh and sway.

With each new path that we create,
Our hearts beat fast; it's never late.
In this whirlwind of joy, we run,
Together forever, only just begun.

Boundless Emotions

In the grand circus of our hearts,
Clowns juggle feelings with silly parts.
Laughter erupts, a joyful refrain,
While love's confetti falls like rain.

Your socks are mismatched, what a delight!
We dance in pajamas, what a sight!
With popcorn in hand, we make merry,
Silly love stories, none too scary.

Whispers of secrets in cozy nooks,
We giggle like children, sharing books.
Inflatable hearts in a bouncy realm,
Where joy is the ship, and we are at the helm.

So let's skip through this whimsical maze,
Chasing each other in love's funny ways.
With each goofy grin and playful tease,
Our boundless emotions are sure to please.

A Fortress of Yearning

In a silly castle of dreams we dwell,
Guarded by giggles, oh what a spell!
The moat is filled with fizzy drinks,
Our love stands tall, or so it seems!

With pillows as shields, we wage a soft war,
Cuddling for comfort, laughter galore.
The banners we wave are made of old sheets,
While tickles and giggles are our favorite feats.

The drawbridge lowers for jokes passed around,
In a kingdom where silliness is truly crowned.
Our hearts play knights, brave and unbowed,
In this fortress of yearning, we laugh out loud.

So let's dance with dragons and play make-believe,
In our whimsical world, we both can achieve.
With each silly armor our spirits take flight,
In this fortress of yearning, everything feels right.

Veils of Understanding

In a funhouse mirror, your face I see,
Each twist and turn, we laugh with glee.
Veils of silliness filter our views,
As we decode each other's funny cues.

With sarcasm winked and puns in tow,
We dance through wittiness, row by row.
Your confusion adds spice to this play,
A tangle of banter that brightens the day.

Sharing our quirks like treasures untold,
Our love is a riddle—yet never too bold.
Between bursts of laughter, we find a new way,
To navigate veils on this delightful ballet.

So let's toast to humor, the secret we share,
Understanding flourishes in joy and in care.
With each witty jibe, we hang on our threads,
In this tapestry of love, where laughter spreads.

Threads of Connection

Like yarn in a basket, we twist and unwind,
Stories and laughter, each thread intertwined.
Our tapestry's wild, with patterns of cheer,
Silly knots tighten when you're near.

With goofy debates on who's the best,
We argue with giggles, it's all just a jest.
In the fabric of friendship, we sew with delight,
Each blunder a stitch, making it bright.

Strumming the heartstrings, a harmonious tune,
We dance 'round the kitchen, love's hectic monsoon.
With cookies that crumble, and sprinkles that spill,
Each tasty disaster is a love-bag filled.

So here's to our threads, each quirky design,
A patchwork of moments, perfectly fine.
In the loom of our lives, we craft and connect,
With laughter as glue, a cherished effect.

The Guardian of Secrets

Whispers hide in the corners,
A sock, a shoe, a missing spoon.
Who took my last slice of cake?
A mystery no one can disprove.

Laughter echoes off the fridge,
Notes scribbled on napkins galore.
A ninja in pajamas sprinting,
Dodging chores like a pro at war.

Tales of mischief shared in jest,
My heart guards secrets with a grin.
Like cats on soft pillows, we jest,
Bonding through chaos we're in.

Love's antics in a silent room,
A giggle fights the stifled gloom.
In moments wrapped in pure delight,
We dance like shadows in the night.

Harmonies of Unspoken Words

We tiptoe through a symphony,
Each look a note that plays so sweet.
The silence hums with laughter held,
As mismatched socks dance on our feet.

Your grin can start a riot loud,
A wink ignites the spark we share.
With secret glances, laughter proud,
The jesters roam without a care.

Like two clowns in a comedy,
Our hearts beat to a silly rhyme.
We stumble through life's grand ballet,
Grasping for joy, stealing time.

In this theater we create,
The audience made of our dreams.
Unspoken words float on the air,
In our duet of giggly schemes.

Portrait of Togetherness

Two peas in a pod, side by side,
Your jokes make even onions weep.
A canvas splashed with spilled ice cream,
Memories we collect and keep.

Propriety takes a silly break,
When you spill coffee on my shirt.
We laugh until we start to shake,
Finding love's humor in the dirt.

Each snapshot framed with goofy grins,
Moments captured, both bright and bold.
In the gallery of our beginning,
Laughter is worth more than gold.

Side by side, we paint the day,
With colors bright, we misbehave.
In the portrait of our lives so fun,
We find a world that we both crave.

Resounding Affection

Your socks do the cha-cha at night,
While I'll serenade the lonely moon.
Harmony in chaos, we fight,
A duet of laughter and cartoon.

Each day, a new comedy sketch,
Playing out with each quirk and flaw.
Bantering like a seasoned pair,
Sharing a life that has no law.

The echoes of our love's delight,
Bouncing off walls, a joyful cheer.
In playful beats, we find the light,
A rhythm that pulls the whole world near.

Hearts that giggle in shady spots,
Our playful jests, a sweet affair.
With every jest that time begot,
Resounding affection fills the air.

www.ingramcontent.com/pod-product-compliance
Lightning Source LLC
Chambersburg PA
CBHW062106280426
43661CB00086B/271